IF THERE WERE WOLVES

IF THERE WERE WOLVES

WOLVES

TIM PRATT

PRIME BOOKS

Thanks to Jay Wentworth and Lynn Doyle, my first best teachers, and to all the editors who published these poems in their original forms.

TABLE

Ts'its'tsi'nako. 9
Dream Sketches. 11
Eight Transformations 13
Visions. 15
While You're in St. Augustine. 18
Holly Grove. 20
Diminishing 23
Intermittence 25
How to Love a Fairy Maid. 30
Other Altars of the Heart 32
Slumbering 35
Ghost. 37
Cupid's Arrows 40
My Night with Aphrodite. 43
Nidhigg 45
Ongoing 47

OF CONTENTS

Early Times 49

The Fey Girl at Home 51

Mask 52

Bacchanal 55

Neither Eat Nor Drink There 57

Forking Paths 60

An Incident in the Country 63

Poor Bahamut 65

Orpheus Among the Cabbages 68

Soul Searching 72

Daughter and Moon 75

Muse Trap 77

Still Life, with Frog 79

Sometimes Another Dream 81

Crossing 82

Talking To Your Sleep 84

Ts'its'tsi'nako

Imagine a woman. Imagine a spider. Imagine
the woman is a spider, but also a woman, and also
imagine that she made everything you see,
and also that she made you, so that you might see
the other things she made. Imagine that she made
your imagination.

Thinking about the thought-spider-woman
leads rapidly to tautological territory; she is
a mirror held up to a mirror held up
to the light flickering on the walls of the cave.

Of course, there are many kinds of spiders,
and of course, she made the many spiders,
the shy ones, the slow-to-anger black widows,
the recluses that kill with bites you never feel,
the orb-spinners, the garden spiders, the harmless
flycatchers that live in the corners of your room.

Imagine that she cannot control her thoughts,
that to imagine is to create, imagine that everything
she imagined came instantly to be. Think about

the experiments done by drugging spiders, and the webs
they made; the obsessive spirals of spiders
on speed, the lazy cat's-cradles of spiders
on THC. Imagine that the world is a series
of webs spun by a woman (who is a spider)
who is imagining herself through a series
of altered states. Is that an explanation
for anything?

Imagine that she imagined
beings that could imagine things themselves.
Imagine that she imagined you.

Imagine the responsibility
that implies.

Dream Sketches

I pour moonlight
in a glass and you laugh
and ask for wine.
I hang my watch
on a branch and you
start a breathy chant
about slaves to marked
time. I take you in
my arms and you slip
away, laughing like
a faun. I braid daisies

in a chain and you wear
them like gold. I sit silent
and alone on a windy
set of steps and you
come for me to have
and hold. I pledge my
heart and soul and you
say you can't give me
both. I sit on a gravel

path and you whisper
a glistening poem in

my ear. I comb the beach
for seashells and meet
you barefoot and halfway.
You have a bucket
of smooth and colored clicking
stones and you hold it
like a bouquet. Your green
dress billows and your face
is like the breaking day.
You say "I'm glad
you came."

Eight Transformations

She drifts through my door
trailing starlight
and the room becomes a temple
for moon-colored gods.

The soft glow
of candlelight
wraps her in a halo

and slow clouds of breath
take the shape
of remembered angels.

Casual gestures become music.

She touches my skin
and the world
unfolds before us.

Every shadow is an invitation.

Her hair falls like fire
into the hearth of my hands.

She slips away
into the rainy dawn
and takes the night
with her.

Visions

She sees visions.
Not real;
not the way a vacuum-cleaner
or a cook-pot
or a bottle of beer is real.

We walk past snapdragons,
she sees real ones,
not peeking from leaves
but buried in earth,
buildings on backs,
gardens on shoulders.

We drive past a bulldozer
toppling a pine and she wails,
tells me she sees a dryad,
arms lopped off,
bleeding on the dirt.
I look.
No blood, no dryad.
Just a bulldozer, blade wet with sap.
I shiver anyway.
All those trees.

She has wings.
I touch her back in love,
during love,
I don't touch wings.
Like a butterfly, she says, and takes my hand.
Here. And here. She presses my palm to air.

She talks to snowflakes.
No two alike?
Maybe a few, she says.

So no, not real, not like a soup can,
a bar of soap, a plot of ground
is real.

Maybe like a rainbow.
You have to stand just right
to see a rainbow,
facing the sun,
the rain a veil before you.

Or northern lights. The natives say
the light can take you,
that it scythes down to earth sometimes,
hungry. They hunker down and hide when
they see the lights.
The cold and the stillness, those are real.

Once we walked down a sunlit street,
she was chattering like a magpie
collecting bright things,
and we passed a shop window
of shining plate glass.
I stopped as she walked on.
I thought I saw something in the glass,
but it must have been the reflection
of a rainbow. Color arcing
from her shoulders
like wings.

While You're in St. Augustine

I'm in Savannah, another place
I've never been with you
(also Bangkok, New Orleans,
and the north side of the moon
where there are galleries
of dust that put SoHo to shame),
sitting in a new chair
in a boxed-in verandah —
can I see the street
through the shutters and the wall,
through sprawling years
of balmy nights, precious ice
and madeira?
In a fresh-painted oblong room,
I think of you.

I feel your flesh and auras
tugging at me. Our lifelines
got tangled some time ago.
I pull those knots,
but you just laugh, make

cat's cradles, jacob's ladders,
hammocks in the air.

I can smell your waters.

I could twist your red hair
in my fingers, and your fingers
in my hand. I want you here,
on the waterfront, posing with the statues
and conversing with gulls
in the language of shared travels.

Instead of always heading south,
ever south,
and me again, falling short.

Holly Grove

She told me it was the oldest grove
of holly trees in the world, or
maybe just the country, I forget
which. "It's two days after midsummer,"
she said, "But close enough for a celebration."

All the mythic elements were there — history
in the fiber of ancient live trees (like that poor girl
who ran from Apollo and, transformed into a laurel,
had to stand still forever just to get away), the stars
pinwheeling slowly through their elaborate
ballroom-dance courses, nude-girl naiads
splashing in the shallow water, and somewhere
a snorting bull roaming the darkness,
deep-chested and archetypal.

There aren't a lot of happily-ever-afters
in those old stories; the gods of the
Mediterranean were too human for those,
too firmly planted in the middle of the world,
for all their Olympian posturing. Love

affairs often ended with people turned
into trees or flowers or lonesome sounds.

(Orpheus was lucky. His lover died before
she could abandon him in a more prosaic
fashion)

(No, that's ridiculously bitter. He wasn't
lucky. He was smashed apart by grief
and furies)

I watched my ex-lover swim
in the moonlight, Psyche to my Cupid,
Helen to my — well, say Faust. I thought
about all the things those long-ago
folk had to endure just to become
constellations.

Let her go, then. I don't want her
to transform herself to escape me,
to be a tree in my backyard. I don't
want her if I have to make bargains
with the lords of the underworld,
or even the dark things in my private
caverns. Let us both live on in the middle
of this Earth, and the middle of our own
stories. You don't always have to fall

apart over love

   falling

     apart.
 I sat on a log by the fire and looked
at the flames and the pale shapes
of the other girls nymphing away in
the two-days-after-midsummer dark,
watching night fall on one mythic time,
but aware always of later chances
to become part of a beautiful
future constellation.

Diminishing

You were my butterfly girl
white-winged and trailing flame
while the flowerbeds burned,
weeping over rare steaks
and empty rainbarrels,
walking roofpeaks like balance beams
and ghosting with the crows.

You were queen of pigeons and sparrows
and you could never rest
on the first floor.
You threw open all my windows,
put plants on the fire escape
and set a place for the moon at dinner.

You told me about monsters
and I read you stories
about gray-eyed girls
and clattering passions and how
to stop a stream in its bed.

You leapt off rocks and crawled
through windows and with every twisted
ankle you grew taller and surer of step
and I fell back, calling, crawling, stopped.

You made masks and paintings
and your eyes glittered
like sapphires or lust.

You spun farther away like satellites
and spiraled to the vanished point.

And, like autumn, you swung round again.

Intermittence

1

I've had enough of sensitivity
and trying to infuse
the whole futile
affair
with magic
(there is passion
but there is also dynamite
and neither is an explosion
in itself).
The fact is you always
get up at four a.m.
to leave
and I always
let you go.

2

You love me and I love you
(and jack and jill went up
the hill to have a pale

encounter) and that's all right.
But it's not enough.

I always fall in love
with the girl in the checkered skirt
or the brunette
behind the coffee shop counter

and you always meet
another mask-maker
who appeals to your sense
of symbols
and maybe gives you orgasms.

It's been two months so far
this time and I
still love you.

I can't tell
if we're fools
or only liars.

3

I don't know
if you could tolerate
the way I go on hands

and knees in used bookstores,
I don't know if I'd like
your cooking or your taste
in couches. I don't know
for sure if I'll ever
see you again, or what
I'll say if I do.
I just hope I can write
a book of poems about it.
I'll send you a copy
for Christmas.
You can use it
to kill spiders.

4

Or maybe I always stay.
I'll be honest. I'm static,
you're dynamic. I cling
and you sparkle.
I'd think following
would appeal to your romantic
side, but you're so
strangely practical at times.
"You're here but where will you sleep
and what will the landlord say
and do you expect me

to pick up your socks?"
You love the way I look
when I'm sleepy and you can't
turn down my omelets,
but one night
and a good breakfast
can only take us so far.

5

So like all the other poems
this one is undone
by history, by the happening-now
sliding relentlessly into
the happened-then,
and I hope you're happy
with your wrought-iron lamps
and your purple rug,
sitting on your make-do bed,
eyes shining, hands clasped,
without me,
and finally as uncrossed
as the stars.

Joy

I don't do anything
these days but I
work and sleep
and in between
I write.
And sometimes
my friend Katherine
comes over and we
sit and eat pistachios
and talk about love.

How to Love a Fairy Maid

If you're jealous, she won't understand. Her heart
beats only a dozen times across your life's
span. If you rage and thunder she will wrinkle
her snow-smooth brow and purse her pretty
mouth. She won't see what all the fuss is about.

She is as old as the stars, and her dreams are wider
than any of yours are. She will never tell you lies — she
doesn't see the use. You will always be burdened by her
bitter truths: that you will live and wilt and die all
in the bloom of her youth. She has loved before
and will again, time after time, without end.

Her patience will try yours — you will feel
like water passing over stone.

Remember that you cool and soothe her.

She will never be mortal, not even for you. If you
ask, she'll smile, inscrutable, and take a nap that lasts
until the fall of empires, until dust is all that's left of you.

If you love her for her wonders, for her wings and green
expanses, her facility with shaping things from bone
and stone and branches, then your chances for happiness
are bare and fleeting. She doesn't need another wide-eyed
    admirer,
and the tubercular poets of old have said it all better than
    you can.

But:

if you can see
to the center of her heart,
where the birth of worlds nestle
and tragedies shudder apart,

then you can love a fairy maid,
but only in her own long way.

Other Altars of the Heart

I'm watching through your window again, my face
against the dirty glass, squinting inward to watch
your progression from love to loneliness to more
final dispositions, and you don't know I'm there.
You are kneeling before a skeleton strung
up on the wall, it is cast in metal, bones
sewn together with thin copper filaments,
arms crossed pharaoh-style over an empty
chest (I don't mean to think of the tin man
but I do; he should have been a sociopath
armed with woodaxe and wit). You are kissing
the feet of the metal man. Your shrine to Aphrodite

is shoved aside, candles burned up and broken, mirror
turned down (a rejection of vanity or self-
reflection?), blue jars spilling their freight of dried
flowers onto your dirty carpet. Your floor
is ankle-deep in shreds of lace and rabbit droppings,
and your broken-necked bunny is clotted with black
flies. There are strange stains on the walls and your terminal
neighbor is wailing in sustained pain from next
door. Love is not a goddess much at home here.

The metal man is a new diversion of the
soul, another god I drove you to. You used
to worship naked but now you are swathed in cotton

and wool, a thick black scarf stifling your hair,
and I grow nervous standing on the sill. You have
turned your will from capricious Venus to a muted
metal shape on the wall, and I imagine
thick dark chains and swaddling cocoons
and the ball gags that always so unnerved
you. I know this god, this is the lord of the vault
of the heart, and as I watch, you sear your many wounds,
your love's amputations, and close your chest tight.
The night is yours now, your mouth is full of silver
teeth and your nails are sharp, your smile is vacant
and winning and you are the bearer of heart's death,

as I have unwittingly been. You dress in leather
and you are supple as molten lead, you
are all hard angles under imagined softness.
I sink from your window, stepping down to the natural
gas tank, down to the weedy gravel pockmark of
your back yard. I hear the pounding wordless music
from the strip club across the street and confuse it
with the beat of my blood. I think of all
the altars that I've led you to. I hope I never
meet you in a bar. You will scatter men like

ashes burned in the blue heart of your sacrificial
fire, constant, untended, without heat.

Slumbering

I dreamed of you last night,
you'd built up your life
from cast-off feathers and baling wire
and smears of cocaine around
your bloody nostrils
and made a radiant woman
of yourself. You'd lost weight
like you always wanted, you crouched
comfortable on the edge of the couch
and talked with delicate flutterings
of delicate fingers. You forgave me.

I waited for the inevitable
nightmare twist, the one raven note
in the bluebird chorus, but it never
came. We walked through blackberries
on the side of the road
and the thorns didn't tear us.
We parted old friends and I felt
the familiar pull of your peculiar
green eyes before I left

and thought "If only — like this —
before." I woke up and the dream

was crowded out by insistent memories,
seeing your mascara smeared,
your face puffy from crying, hearing
the raucous bitter laugh you cawed
when I told you about the other
woman (again), remembering second-hand
tales of one-night stands and spiraling
depression and ever more drugs.
I remembered slipping thieflike
from the dark of your bedroom,
my pants in one hand, creeping

by the slumbering dragon
of our just-passed love. Another
dream crumbled at waking. I'd like
to believe in visions, in celestial
communications, but my dream was just
a wish I think, and somewhere
right now you're rolling out of a strange
bed, mussed as a mound of dirty clothes,
taking a moment to hate me,
or, worse yet, never thinking
about me at all.

Ghost

The sorcerer got home from his job
at the 7-11 and stood limp in the center
of his empty bedroom, reading runes
in the fine traceries of dust. The blurry
portents gave him only old news:

She's gone.

The collected fragments of two years'
love jeered at him from shelves, desks,
and his bedside table. An origami rose
she'd folded for him one night during
her Japan phase, wearing a silk kimono
and smoking on the bed. A silver armband
filigreed and coiled, resting without
even the ghost of a limb inside. A stuffed
dog, one-eyed and grinning (idiotically
he thought now, or rabidly) given
two Valentine's past.

         He gathered
the gifts and pictures and arranged them

on the green–gold floor. He took
a forgotten dress, wine-stained and balled
in a closet corner, and spread it
on the carpet. He placed her stuffed
hedgehog at the head, a mismatched pair
of woolen socks at the feet, a scattering
of rings and bracelets beneath the sleeves.
He arrayed the remainder in a loose circle.

His fingers trembled. These sweet
mementos had become swiftly humming
engines of grief. He lit a scented candle
(her favorite, "Rainforest Dawn") and conjured.
His hands moved, sticky with cola and reeking
of dollar bills.

          He drew the spirit of past
love from the stuffed dog, the tarnished rings,
the fragile rose. The dog shriveled into
a raisin shape, the rose blackened, and rings
dissolved to silver dust as the dress swelled,
filled with ghost hips,

                    ghost breasts,

                            ghost legs.

But the dress sagged, and flattened with a sound
of sighing breath. The sorcerer slumped, hands

unmoving, eyes down. Perhaps, he thought, if she'd
died, and I could have grabbed her ghost — but no.
She'd only stopped loving him, and moved away,
and the phantom past had faded

> too far to be saved.

Cupid's Arrows

There's Cupid out on Williams street
dressed in a blood-dappled toga
with sandals made
of tongues and leather. He's collecting
potion-parts, crawling through alleyways
and dim bars, sniffing for the scent
of hot flesh and listening
for desperate whispers
and ripping zippers.

He picks up an old condom,
torn and left in the park
the night before
and tosses it in his bag.
He takes a tissue, wadded full
of jerkjuice, from a garbage
can. He goes
through the neighbor's
garbage and peruses
blurred pornography
from the nineteen-seventies.

He takes the decorations,
runs his blunt sticky fingers
over lace panties, sex toys
with dead batteries,
a box of chocolate
or a withered bouquet
if he's feeling especially sublime.

He snaps a garter and hears
the music of love. He watches
videos, rented furtively
late at night on the far side
of town. Cupid takes notes.

He mixes the carefully collected
vials of semen (spat out by housewives
with delicate stomachs)
and the blood (from virgins,
menstruation, and anal penetrations)
and strands of hair
(stuck to hot pillows, pulled out
in tight fistfulls),
and warm oils, whipped cream,
chocolate sauce, Vaseline
and saliva (dripped
from rote-impassioned lips)
into his cauldron.

He simmers over low heat
and dips his arrowheads
into the potion.
It is the opposite
of poison
(he thinks).
He fills his quiver
with sympathetic magic
and barbed points,
he tells us "This is love."

And we, pierced through
heart and loins,
believe him.

My Night with Aphrodite

I met Aphrodite in a bar and picked
her up (I asked her sign and she showed
me her constellation — you know what
starry nights do to women). We went
back to my place and had a few drinks
and went to bed. She was perfect, tongue
like honey, body like love, and she said
all the right things. I was done in no time
(she is a goddess) but I helped finish her off.

In the morning she was still perfect. My breath
tasted sour and she flinched away when I went
to peck her cheek. I pissed and shaved and she
watched like somebody seeing a snake eat
a rat for the first time. I sucked in my
stomach, brushed my hair, took a shower.

She followed me to the kitchen and didn't
want breakfast. She gagged at the smell
of frying sausage. She was still naked.
Her breasts defied gravity. I was hungover
and felt like dogshit on a bootheel. I noticed

that her feet didn't touch the floor. She
suggested that I could be a better housekeeper,
wrinkling her pretty nose at the dishes in my sink.

I walked her to the door. She didn't want
a ride. My car, she said, smelled like cigarettes
and fast food. She would fly. "You can
call me if you want," she said doubtfully.
"Just light a white candle, scented with
rose and jasmine, and invoke my name five—"

"Sure," I said, and closed the door.

Nidhigg

It has been said that everyone is a world unto themselves,
and to stretch a metaphor, that implies
subterranean depths, and biological equivalents
to geological structures, and at least the possibility
that myths about the world might apply
on a more personal level as well.

Consider the corpse-grinder, monster of the North,
dragon of envy, a beast with the jewels of dead warriors
adorning its teeth, with scales as milky white
as permafrost, who lives beneath the Earth
and gnaws forever at the roots
of the tree of the world, constantly killing
the living thing from which all
existence grows. Take a short leap
and imagine your brainstem, your spine, your nerves
growing through your own firmament like roots. Imagine
the world tree of your life, and think
of the caverns beneath the meat, the dark places
within you, the taproots growing
down through treasure caverns, Morlock holes,
abandoned bunkers, through underground

lakes filled with the blind cave fish
of your lesser impulses. Does a dragon live there,
gnawing at the endings of your nerves, shitting
in your stillest waters, eating the corpses
of your memories, poisoning your wells?

Everyone is a world. There are monsters
beneath the world. Apply the transitive property
and consider the results.

Ongoing

I don't need openings, which
come so easily: leaning
together on balconies, eyes
meeting across a crowded
laundromat.

Nor endings. I have collected
a number of interesting
revelations, which I keep
in a black notebook on
a string around my neck. I understand
deathbed confessions and the sweet
illogic of happy endings,
which is nothing more than choosing
the perfect moment to look away.

It is these middles that trouble
me, these long days in
March when things are well-
settled, food in the cupboard,
money in the bank, love
and art in good proportion,

my heart full
of inexplicable yearnings.

So many nights I go
out walking in search
of connection, and so often
I find it: someone sitting
on a bench beneath a thorn
tree, a yellowing paperback
left out on the steps.

But these too pass, and none
of it finishes my life
with the closure of a
book. I never encounter
a line of asterisks when
I enter the bedroom or
the hospital, I never
faint when things
are at their worst.

Turn the page. I'll still
be here, working through
the permutations,
skipping ahead to try
last lines, or turning back
to review my best beginnings.

Early Times

This is a morning clouded
with visions or maybe
only rain. You're sleeping on
the loveseat, where you've been
the only one for a while. That old
brown blanket is wrapped around
you like a threadbare shroud, you
are huddled and singular. Your hair
is a spreading shadow of unruly
black, and when your eyes open
they seem blurred and drowning. I
think you've been crying but you're
only sick. You haven't cried in
ages.

    There's a difference between
being lonely and being alone, and
you've been both. You're having
a rough couple of weeks and one
of them hasn't started yet. You were
up with the rainy dawn today and
wandering, watching the scenes change
on the stage of the same old play.

Now
you're back, crashed low and somehow
laughing at the state of things. The only
way you can stand my company is by
ignoring my essential optimism. But just
for a minute you take my side, you say
"There was a moment when the sun
broke from the clouds and the whole
mountain was lit from behind, it was like
smiling back at God."
I'm not worried
about you. You'll find another angel.

The Fey Girl at Home

When I try to imagine
what she must go home to
I think of wicker trunks
and polished blue bottles,
earthenware jars
on groaning shelves
and high dark rafters
filled with the twitter
of birds,
leaded glass windows
and tarnished mirrors
and lanterns on the stairs.
But she probably has
a beanbag chair
and a threadbare couch
and a ginger cat
that used to be a stray.
Wherever she lays her head
is a house of wonders
just the same.

Mask

Feathers and paint, kohl sticks and smeared
pigments, cerulean blue beads, scales
and links of chain mail heaped on a rough
wooden table in a narrow room, four
hurricane lamps lighting it up. This is
the maskmaker's workshop on the avenue
of greater dreaming, a place only open
at night.

I have come to find a new
face and body, a truer expression
than the one I see in the mirror. Here is
the Lakota ghost shirt, feathered and white
and clacking, and stone jars of pale
face paint. Here is the zippered leather
mask of a fetishist; it gives me a chill
because I think it can only destroy
identity, not reveal a deeper one. I move on, to
Carnival masks, a crocodile headdress I linger
over but know is not mine, a harlequin's
cloth face of fixed hilarity, a beautiful

smooth gold mask of the sun. These all have
power, but none are mine.

Then the maskmaker
enters, a lush woman serene and regal as
the moon, her eyes blue and lively behind
a simple silver domino mask. "You want
to be a serpent," she says, picking up
a length of python skin and putting it down
again. "Or an angel, above everything." She lets
white silk run through her fingers. "Or
a manitou, with a face that shifts like the sky or
water, changing to fit your needs." She shakes
her head.

"But you are not those things." She lifts
a bundle wrapped in gray cobwebs. "You are a
spider. Lonely architect. Thought-maker. Weaver.
Moving in two worlds. Poison-head." She unwraps
the webbing. I see segmented legs, glossy
black mandibles, and something scuttles under
the trapdoor of my heart. Not a lion, then, or
an eagle, but this feels right. She holds out the spider
mask, sticky filaments still trailing, and eases it
onto my face. I see with spider's eyes, geometry
and possibility and vibrations in the air, corners

and spirals and prey. The legs on the mask wrap
tightly around my head and I

wake in my dusty bedroom,
looking at the corners where the ceiling meets
the walls, thinking

"I've never noticed how much
a spider's eyes resemble diamonds."

Bacchanal

Your party is getting out of hand. The frat boys become
satyrs, but they brought the kegs and the pretty girls so
you can't complain. There's no food, really, but you can take
    fruit
from the trees. The cheerleaders take off their sweaters and
    turn
into nymphs. Somebody throws up in your shower, but it's
only Bacchus, so that's all right. Eventually the
water turns to beer and then to piss, and the resident
sorcerer mumbles something about alchemy and fondles
the dryad who lives in the book case. Your dog looks like a

basilisk and he's trying to turn your oblivious
cat to stone. Your bedroom door is closed but you hear the
heavy breathy sounds of occupation from the other
side. It sounds like Bacchus and at least three nymphs and you
    don't
see that sheep who was hanging around the kitchen earlier.
You're getting pissed and wondering if you have any clean
    sheets.
Nope. The satyrs are using them for togas. All the nymphs

are taken, and this palace doesn't even look like your

place anymore, so you can't throw anyone out. You go

outside for some air and hear singing. You follow the sound

to a gold and marble fountain where your patio

table used to be. There's a blonde dressed in sea foam and

clouds in the water, singing a wordless song. You can just

make out that she used to be that girl who works at the

library. You went out with her once. Now she's looking

at you, smiling, and you realize she's a siren and

she's drawing you in. You can faintly tell you're doomed but

    that's

all right. You were beginning to think she'd never call back.

Neither Eat Nor Drink There

She invited me to her house
for dinner, and her kitchen
was a surprise. I'd never seen
a fireplace as big as a garage
before, especially not in a third-
floor apartment. She said
it was meant for roasting
whole oxen, and I said "Oh,"
though that didn't explain
the chains, caked with ash
and grease, dangling from
the bricks inside.

(She had black hair soft as old
leather; or red like fragments
of a broken taillight flashing
in the sun; or yellow as
fish scales in a dream;
or something; it's honestly
quite a blur)

There were servants who glided
silently around with bottles of
wine and trays of appetizers,
but whenever I glimpsed
them on the periphery
they seemed made of moss
and old sticks lashed together
with twine, or else like lumps
of river clay.

She took my hand and led me
to the table, put a golden dish
in front of me, piled high
with pasta, but it smelled
like a plate full of bitter greens.

I almost ate anyway. Then
she said "Wait," and took
an old peppermill, large
and heavy as a scepter,
and cranked.

Pepper sifted down, like ashes,
black snow, the space
between the stars somehow
powdered. And when I looked
at her face it was all curves

and reflections, smooth
and white as molded
plastic, and I knew (more
than ever) that nothing
was quite what it seemed.

I excused myself, hurried
for the front door, but the halls
go on and on, and I think I've
been here for days. Lately
I've been hiding in the guest
bathroom, sitting on a toilet
made of glass, sleeping in an
onyx tub. There is a slow
knocking in the pipes,
and somewhere, far off, I think
I hear an oven door being opened
and closed over and over,
and what could be weeping
or just a slow, sad song
of loss.

Forking Paths

The god of the crossroads came to me
in a shabby café in Missouri, during
a time of confusion and malaise — a
personal infestation of spiritual lice,

a hundred chigger bites on the flesh
of my sense of purpose, you might say.
The god rode in the head of my coffee
server, a displaced punkette with

mismatched eyes and buzzed-black
hair and a silver ring in her left
nostril. I recognized the god's arrival
by the usual signs — the scent of copper

and vanilla in the latté steam, the jingle
of the bells hung on the door like
garlands, the revving and honking
and backfiring of cars in the street

trying to go every direction at once
and tearing themselves apart in the process.

"You're waiting again," the god said in
the punkette's sexy-raspy voice. "What

are you waiting for?"
"I can't do it all," I said, stirring
cold coffee with my forefinger. "I hate
to make decisions I can't revise

later. I used to take comfort in quantum
uncertainty and the many-worlds theory,
the idea that somewhere else, some other
me was doing everything." The god

snorted and said "Every other you is sitting
in this stupid coffee shop with the water-
stained walls and the rude waitstaff, or else
crouching by a rock staring at a stream, or looking

up at a flyspecked motel ceiling — and all of you
are getting yelled at by me." The god came around
the counter and thumped me in the chest. I
gasped as my heart sputtered, stuttered,
stopped

and then started again as all the engines
outside revved and the cars surged

forward. "Every road ends," the punkette
god said. "You can't linger

forever." Her mismatched eyes were one
color now, the morning blue of a sky
I once saw in Georgia, and I wondered
how many dawns and journeys I had left.

The god departed, and I whispered
my thanks to the punkette,
pushed back from the table, stood up,
and walked into the remaining

hours and miles of my life.

An Incident in the Country

Two days ago it rained fish
from a clear sky,
all kinds, silver slick and shiny,
big and small with bulgy eyes
and sharp and tiny teeth.
They shattered on tombstones
and fence posts and chimneys
and car hoods and spattered
innards all over,
and the barefoot poor kids
scooped them up to take home
to their dishwater moms for dinner.
Everyone else shut themselves
inside and watched from windows
as minnows bounced on mailboxes
and jellyfish broke open
on tin roofs for three straight hours.
For the past two days frowning
big-shouldered men
with plugs in their noses
have been shoveling fish
into wheelbarrows, dump trucks,

and little red wagons
as they gag in the sun.
But one fish fell
in my full rain-barrel,
a big one with whiskers
and great green eyes,
swimming lazy as I feed him
bits of his brothers
and he grows.
Maybe someday
he'll tell me secrets.

Poor Bahamut

Poor Bahamut, the bright fish
of celestial size, swimming
through the coldest depths
of space, dry, among the shoals
of distant stars and heaving
clouds of dust,

with his elephant's
head, his trunk rainbow-scaled
and probing the emptiness before
him; eyes vast as the hearts
of galaxies,

his back an expanse
of sand that beggars
the Sahara, and standing
in the sand a bull as big
as Jupiter, ruminant, stupid.
And on the bull's back
a ruby, its red gleam
just a fragment of the

spectrum of Bahamut's
shining scales.

Poor Bahamut; as if that weight
were not enough, the ruby
in turn supports an angel
with skin like pale marble
and art deco wings;
and that angel holds
long poles upon which spin
six hells (of fire, snow, oil,
suffocation, biting flies,
and ennui), and upon his head
the angel holds the Earth,
and over that (up on a system
of staggered platforms) rest
seven heavens, each with palaces
of platinum and gold.

The world-fish,
carrying the crushing weight
of every human and divine
concern, his spine bowing
under the burden; and though
his brain is larger than
constellations, he is no smarter
than any fish in a bowl.

Poor Bahamut lives in a perpetual
present, a now of pain
and weight, swimming into nothing
from nothing, the whole world
above him, out of sight.

Orpheus Among the Cabbages

She picked up a pomegranate, squeezed
it hard, sighed. She'd always preferred golden
delicious apples, but they were all
mushy today. Someone called out
from the direction of the cabbages,
not her name, just pleading. She pushed
her clattering cart toward the greenest
part of the produce department.

A man's head rested among the cabbages.
He had black hair, and the kind of olive skin that
some women find exotic when they don't know
better. "I am Orpheus," he said, "cursed to live
forever, bereft of love, and now left
among these living green things
that by their fecundity mock my living
death. My woe is legend . . . "

She resisted the urge to thump
his forehead like a melon. She called
to a beefy old man wearing a

supermarket smock. "What's this head
doing in among the cabbages?" she asked.

He walked toward her, looked at Orpheus,
grunted. "I just unload the crates," he
said. "The quality of the vegetables
is none of my business."

"Did these cabbages come from Greece?"
she asked.

"Olives are what come from Greece," he
said. "Cabbages come from places like
Ohio." He wandered away.

"Long I sought my love," Orpheus said.
"Long I wandered singing in
the lands below the earth."

She looked at the sign. "Cabbages, 89 cents
a head." She picked up Orpheus by his
hair. He didn't seem to mind. If his neck
had been bloody she might have left
him there, but his wound was smooth
as cut cucumber. She dropped him
in her basket, paid for him at the register,

thinking "Of all the places to find
true love."

In the car, on the way home, Orpheus went
on and on about his dead wife from inside
the grocery bag.

She wished he would stop; a girl could
start to feel like an afterthought. She decided
he would never love her after all.

A mile from her house he started singing.
She wept. So did a dog in the street, a mailman
passing by, and a stop sign. She decided to keep
him after all.

When she got home she put the rest
of the groceries away, but took Orpheus
into her dusty bedroom, swinging him
gently by his hair. "Long I sought my love,
and an end to loneliness," Orpheus said.
"Long I searched to find the gates
of my paradise denied."

She undressed, surprised to find
herself trembling. She stretched out
on the bed and bent her knees, then

tucked the murmuring head of Orpheus
between her thighs.

"Sing out," she said, and he did.

A bit later, so did she.

Soul Searching

On weekends I help my old neighbor look
for his soul. He says he used to be a wizard, or a giant
(the story varies from telling to telling), and, as was
the custom for his kind, he put his soul into an egg
(or perhaps a stone) for safe-keeping. He hid the egg
(or stone) inside a duck (or in the belly
of a sheep, or in a tree stump), and so long
as his soul was safe, his body could not be killed
or wounded. "Oh," he says. "I was the greatest
terror of the hills. I ate the hearts of knights,"
or sometimes, "I lived in my high
tower and none dared oppose me, and with the wave
of my hand I could turn stone to mud
and water to boiling blood."

Or sometimes "The earth trembled
with my every step." He says this
almost wistfully.

My neighbor is seventy at least, I think,
or older (unless he is hundreds of years old
as he claims). His skin is covered in dark freckles,

liver spots, and moles, and he says that each
blemish marks a year he's lived beyond
his rightful span. All he wants is to find the egg
(or stone) that houses his soul, so that he
may break the egg (or crush the stone) and die.

I asked him once, while we looked for his soul
in the garbage cans at the park, "How
could you misplace your soul?"
"I hid it so well, I forgot
where it was hidden," he said.

"Seems like a hell of a thing
to forget," I said.

"When you don't have a soul,"
he said,
"It's harder to know which things
are important
to remember."

We go out every weekend. He's old.
I live alone. We are companions
for one another. He tells marvelous
stories. I think he must have once
taught mythology, though he tells

the tales of gods and heroes
as if he saw it all firsthand.

Once he found a robin's egg
on the ground. It must have fallen
from a nest. He held the egg
in trembling hands, cracked it,
and yolk spilled out. No soul.

He shook the egg
off his hands. Bits of shell
fell to the ground. He wiped
his hands on his pants
and went on looking, picking
up rocks, dropping them
in disgust and frustration.

We go out every weekend,
we walk the length of the town
and back, but somehow
the earth never trembles.

Daughter and Moon

The moon disappeared last week and the world is shuddering
like a wet cat. Cows are sleeping badly and the milk
is sour. The tides have gone insane, arriving and departing
without reason, like a secret alcoholic with a part-time job.
Blood
is flowing (or not flowing) in unusual ways, streams
rush uphill and lovers bicker on park benches everywhere.

The moon is in my house. It is no bigger than a dinner plate
or a basketball, and it is much grittier than it appears in the sky.
My daughter says she lured it with a trail of jelly beans (no
black ones) and that it will go home when it gets bored.
Meanwhile it eats the fresh butter, nestles in the bathtub,
rolls across the shag rug and chases our dog, who howls.

The farmers don't know when to plant. Our president
suspects the Arabs. Dubious astronomers check and re-check
foolproof instruments. People on the street shout that the end
is near, but the economy has never been better. All the spells
chanted under the dark of the moon are coming undone. My
daughter dresses our satellite in bonnets and her dead mother's
scarves.

Today I asked her (she is nine, she has pig-tails and crooked
teeth) what it all means, why the moon came to us, and she
laughed. She ran down the hillside this morning
and the moon floated behind her. They play tag like old
    friends.
My daughter will never be this young again. I wonder
if the moon is telling her secrets. I suspect that it is.

Muse Trap

My muse escaped last week,
slipped out the window between
the bars with my overnight
bag in her hand. I called the police
but they didn't care about a petty
thief, and they said she was too old
to put on a milk carton, so I've
had to resort to other means.

Tonight I made a muse trap
baited with all her favorite
things. I left a trail of palm fronds
and cinnamon sticks and jelly beans
and peacock feathers and moon rocks
and lizard's feet and uncooked meat
and colored glass and weathervanes
and window frost and broken kites
and a book of Yeats and a dish of cream
and a pile of dates and a sprig
of mistletoe sharpened at both ends
and an aloe plant and a glass of the wind
and a star in a blue bottle and a newborn

kitten and an elephant's tusk and chocolate
covered cherries and pears and ripe berries
and three feet of knotted black thread
and a blue silk pillow to rest her head

all leading from my big backyard
through the patio doors to this cardboard
box open wide on the floor. I'm hiding
behind the bathroom door with a knobby
club of fresh-cut oak and a burlap sack
and a music box that plays "Hush Little
Baby" when you open it up. I'll be writing
again by morning if the gods give me luck.

Still Life, with Frog

My friends back in Raleigh
had a chipped ceramic planter
shaped like a frog, and
it rested on their beer-
can-cluttered coffee table
like the presiding deity
in a temple to squalor.

They used the frog for an ashtray,
tossing smoldering butts into
its comically outsized
and gaping mouth.

One night a show came on
the Discovery channel, and they
were too stoned to change it,
so I watched, and learned all
about Tlaltecuhtli,

the gigantic frog-
monster of Aztec mythology,
with fangs like sickles,

and a vast mouth
that served incidentally
as the gateway to the land
of the dead.

That's the night
I gave up smoking,
but even now, when I think
of someday dying,
I see a chipped green
mouth full of ashes,
venting smoke,
and the painted plaster eyes
of the inevitable.

Sometimes Another Dream

Bending the dream we find
prose angels —
ghosts, stories, true
if not historical,
desperately hoping
for a vivid absurdity.

Remembering the world paints
a montage
of transitional fairy
tales, invented relationships,
spiraling frenzies and
serious repetitions.

We live the idiom,
drunken and provocative,
the tongue of fiction
a careful maxim
revealing a hallway.
We return to music.

Crossing

I'll tell you how to make
a raft to cross this river

Collect bones.

You know how bones like to hide
in the grass, in the flesh,
but there's no other way.

Light ones are the best,
bird bones, the hollow ones,
but those are not strong.
It takes a hundred hollow bones
to make a raft.

Pull out your hair
one strand at a time.
If your hair is not long
let it grow. Be patient.
The river will wait.

Bind up the bones
with hair
and make them tight.
Make a space large enough
for yourself to sit
cross-legged.

When a strand breaks,
replace it the next day.
Do not rush;
it takes a long time
to cross this river.

When your raft is done,
a hundred bones bound
by your own thread,
you can cross the river
at twilight.

Or break the raft,
scatter bones
and make fire of your hair.

Talking To Your Sleep

I never noticed how large this room looks
when all the chairs are empty, without
jazz bubbling through the speakers, without
the smell of burnt popcorn wafting through
the air. Here in the last cavity of night
there's nothing but me, sitting Indian-style
on the carpet, and you, breathing rhythmic
as tides on the couch. There's only a candle
burning and I blow that out. This is a place
between blinkings, waiting for the light to come on.

                    It has never been
               harder. It has never been
more important.

In the dark I tell stories to your sleep,
I describe the scuttling, pincered thing
that crawled from the outhouse, the pegasus
grazing in the turnips with the wild deer,
the angels of discrimination come to punish
the ordinary, the blue diamond in the bottom
of the cereal box. I can't tell if I touch

your dreams. Nothing comes out whole;
these visions are like broken cookies at the
bottom of the bag: sweet, but not complete.

                    If only you were
          listening. If only you were
willing to wait.

If you were awake, if we were huddled around
a fire forging legends out of burned leaves
and bared wishes, these stories could keep the wolves
away (if there were wolves). But shards
of story told to the dark, with an audience
of empty chairs, offer no protection.
Still: Spinning. A cat and a golden shroud.
A love story about blackbirds. Beginning with a whim
to end with a whimper. A picture made of scars.

                    There will always be another
          morning. There will always be another
chance to tell it right.
                    You won't always be sleeping.

PUBLICATION HISTORY

"Ts'its'tsi'nako" in *Strange Horizons*, May 2003.

"Dream Sketches" in *Love*, January 2003.

"Eight Transformations" in *Love*, January 2003.

"Visions" in *Star*Line*, January/February 2000.

"While You're in St. Augustine" in *Recursive Angel*, Fall 1998.

"Holly Grove" in *Dark Illuminati* 0, August 2002.

"Diminishing" in *Jabberwocky* 2.

"Intermittence" is original to this collection.

"Joy" is original to this collection

"How To Love A Fairy Maid" in *The Magazine of Speculative Poetry*, February 2003.

"Other Altars of the Heart" in *Jabberwocky* 1.

"Slumbering" is original to this collection.

"Ghost" in *Electric Wine*, Summer 2000.

"Cupid's Arrows" in *Recursive Angel*, May 1999.

"My Night With Aphrodite" in *Asimov's*, January 2003.

"Nidhigg" in *Strange Horizons*, April 2003.

"Ongoing" is original to this collection.

"Early Times" is original to this collection.

"The Fey Girl at Home" is original to this collection.

"Mask" in *Strange Horizons*, June 2001.

"Bacchanal" in *Asimov's*, April, 2001.

"Neither Eat Nor Drink There" in *The Modern Art Cave*, October/November 2002.

"Forking Paths" as "The God of the Crossroads" in *Strange Horizons*, March 2001.

"An Incident in the Country" as "Incident" in *Asimov's*, July 2001.

"Poor Bahamut" in *Strange Horizons*, April 15, 2002.

"Orpheus Among the Cabbages" in *Strange Horizons*, October 2001.

"Soul Searching" in *Strange Horizons*, July 2004.

"Daughter and Moon" in *Weird Tales*, Summer 2001 (issue 324).

"Muse Trap", *Strange Horizons*, February 2002.

"Still Life with Frog" in *Asimov's*, November 2003.

"Sometimes Another Dream" is original to this collection.

"Crossing" in *Appalachian Broadsides*, Spring 1998.

"Talking to Your Sleep" is original to this collection.